Explode The Code® 2nd Edition   5

Essential lessons for phonics mastery

Nancy Hall • Rena Price

EDUCATORS PUBLISHING SERVICE
Cambridge and Toronto

Cover art: Hugh Price
Text illustrations: Laura Price, Alan Price, Kelly Kennedy

Printed in Mayfield, PA, in December 2022
ISBN 978-0-8388-7805-7

9 10 11 12 PAH 25 24 23 22

Lesson 1

The ending *-ed* usually means that something has already happened. If the root ends in *d* or *t*, *-ed* says /ed/ as in add__ed__.

$$\rightarrow \quad +\frac{\frac{2}{2}}{4}$$

Read, write, and ◯ it.

listed __listed__			
heated			
painted			
trotted			
spotted			
melted			
toasted			

The ending *-ed* usually means that something has already happened. If the root ends in *d* or *t*, *-ed* says /ĕd/ as in add*ed*.

$$\rightarrow + \frac{\frac{2}{2}}{4}$$

⬭ the word that matches the picture.

roasted or (rested)?

sanded or slanted?

acted or coasted?

listed or lifted?

weeded or waited?

hunted or handed?

crusted or rusted?

nested or needed?

	Spell.		Write.
$\rightarrow +\dfrac{\begin{array}{r}2\\2\end{array}}{4}$	red (add)	ish (ed)	**added**
	toast tank	ed ful	_____
	self melt	ed ish	_____
	spit spot	est ted	_____
	paint pain	ful ed	_____
	hand hunt	ful ed	_____
	lift fast	ed est	_____

3

Yes or no?

	Yes	No
If you nailed a door closed, could it be opened?	☐	☒
Have robins ever nested in a wastebasket?	☐	☐
Would you have grinned if your cream puff melted?	☐	☐
If you added cheese to bread, would you have a salad?	☐	☐
Would a grasshopper feel fine if it rested all day?	☐	☐
Would you tremble if you were hunted by a wicked robot?	☐	☐
Would you be unhappy if your coat got spattered with paint?	☐	☐

⬭ the word that matches the picture.

crested (feasted) fainted	rusted rested nested
planner planted painted	blister twister misted
roasted boasted fastest	pretend present printed
brainy bridle braided	riddle richest risked
trotted trombone trailer	toasted loafers coasted

5

Pick the best word to finish each sentence.

invented	demanded	expected
pretended	infected	protected
collected	~~shivered~~	inspected

Mel **shivered** in the cold hallway.

If you are feeling sick, you may be _____ with a virus.

The batter wore a helmet that _____ him from a wild pitch.

The fastest pony is _____ to be the winner.

The students _____ stamps and put them in albums.

Seth wore the funny costume when he _____ to be a clown.

The electric wires must be _____ to see if they are safe to use.

X it.

The silly player batted with a twisted tail pipe.	☐	
The helpful player toasted the frosted buns.	☐	
The deep snow melted on the sandy beach.	☐	
The hot sun melted the frosty snowman.	☐	
The twins hunted in the treetop for the lost kitten.	☐	
The twins hunted in the mist, trying to locate the hidden cave.	☐	
Mr. Baird invented a way to grow a candy tree.	☐	
The cats spotted a rat in the hole.	☐	
Walter demanded his supper in a bowl.	☐	
The clowns sang as they lifted the prize painting.	☐	
Debby sketched and painted a model.	☐	
Debby blended milk and eggs and then added nutmeg.	☐	
The tiger spotted a cool spot in the grass.	☐	
Rachel stared at and selected a velvet coat.	☐	

Write it, using a word with -ed at the end.

	listed
	_____
$+ \dfrac{2}{\dfrac{2}{4}}$	_____
	_____
	_____
	_____
	_____

8

Lesson 2

The ending -ed usually means that something has already happened. Sometimes -ed says /t/ or /d/ as in fix<u>ed</u> and play<u>ed</u>.

Read, write, and ⬭ it.

fished _____			
dropped _____			
snowed _____			
yanked _____			
fixed _____			
rocked _____			
spilled _____			

9

The ending -ed usually means that something has already happened. Sometimes -ed says /t/ or /d/ as in fix**ed** and play**ed**.

◯ the word that matches the picture and ◯ the sound -ed makes. The first one is done for you.

tricked or (stained)? t or (d)?	rammed or rained? t or d?
crashed or asked? t or d?	tracked or stacked? t or d?
stained or sailed? t or d?	jumped or lumped? t or d?
planned or played? t or d?	chipped or chilled? t or d?

10

	snore snow	er ed	_____
	fast fish	ed est	_____
	sail sad	ness ed	_____
	plat play	ter ed	_____
	rock rob	ed ber	_____
	six fix	ish ed	_____
	damp jump	ed est	_____

11

Yes or no?

	Yes	No
Could an octopus be trained to eat with chopsticks?	☐	☐
Would a hundred hot dogs tumble if you stacked them up?	☐	☐
Would you be cheerful if a kitten spilled your pudding?	☐	☐
Would you be thanked if you played tennis with the coach's clipboard?	☐	☐
If you tripped on a skunk, would you be smelly?	☐	☐
Would you smile if you discovered a trunk filled with silver?	☐	☐
Can a leaky hose be fixed with tape?	☐	☐

the word that matches the picture.

bumped dampest dumped	slipper slapped slanted
smiling smelly spelled	hopped mopped moaned
dished biked dashed	cleanest chained claimed
dumped pumped pamper	sixteen matched mixed
fasted fastest feasted	mowed snowed moaner

13

Pick the best word to finish each sentence.

opened	traveled	vanished
spattered	hammered	buttered
relaxed	bothered	delayed

Jan dropped the brush, and paint _____ on the rug.

The class planned a bus trip and _____ to three states.

When I am swinging in a hammock, I feel _____.

They gathered a pile of nails and _____ them into the boards.

She ripped off the paper and _____ the box of candy.

Chad toasted the muffin and then _____ it and ate it.

The clever dragon rose in a puff of smoke and _____.

14

X it.

The rowboat was filled with hundreds of seashells.	☐	
Tommy fished from the rowboat and pulled up a rusted can.	☐	
The king was upset when he lost his bat.	☐	
Five rabbits sailed to the sea in a bathtub.	☐	
The class played a game, and one kid tripped and fell.	☐	
Hank and his tame tiger were dressed as twins.	☐	
A black crow snatched a cap from the fat pitcher.	☐	
The player pitched a fast one to the scarecrow.	☐	
Roseanne rocked in a plastic chair while eating peaches.	☐	
Roseanne banged on the big drum.	☐	
The chipmunks asked the acrobats to play leapfrog.	☐	
The chimpanzee will pinch the banana to see if it is ripe.	☐	
Rufus sprayed the mule that was bothered by the heat.	☐	
Rufus traveled by mule when he felt lazy.	☐	

Write it, using a word with -*ed* at the end.

	_____
	_____
	_____
	_____
	_____
	_____
	_____

16

Lesson 3

-*all* says /all/ as in *ba**ll***.
-*alk* says /awk/ as in *wa**lk***.

Read, write, and ⬭ it.

tall _____			
wall _____			
chalk _____			
fall _____			
hall _____			
talk _____			
stall _____			

-all says /all/ as in *b<u>all</u>*.
-alk says /awk/ as in *w<u>alk</u>*.

◯ the word that matches the picture.

calf   or   call?

tail   or   tall?

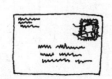

mail   or   mall?

ail   or   all?

stack   or   stalk?

small   or   smell?

hall   or   hill?

chalk   or   check?

Spell.   Write.

	t f	a ee	ll t	_____
	m w	e a	lk lt	_____
	t l	ai a	lk l	_____
	s c	a oa	st ll	_____
	h n	o a	ll lk	_____
	sh ch	e a	lf lk	_____
	st sm	a ea	k ll	_____

Yes or no?

	Yes	No
Can you put all of the spelling list on the chalkboard?	☐	☐
Will the girl get a talking-to for losing tennis balls?	☐	☐
Can a scarecrow use a walky-talky to call its pals?	☐	☐
Is a baseball much smaller than a tall camel?	☐	☐
Did the pony put wallpaper on the sides of its stall?	☐	☐
Would you see twenty tall beasts walking in the hallway?	☐	☐
Will we all have fun walking to the mall to get lemonade?	☐	☐

the word that matches the picture.

calling falling fallow	basement blackball baseball
chuckle chalkboard chocolate	stalks sneakers speakers
hallway overall halting	snuffle snowfall slowdown
walking cactus calling	spitball talking-to telegram
sneaking smelling smallness	walked talked winked

21

Pick the best word to finish each sentence.

taller	smallest	walky-talky
hallway	basketball	chalky
walking	overalls	wallpaper

The baby wore muddy _____ to play in the puddle.

Walking quickly up the _____ gets you to class on time.

With a _____ you can chat with a classmate who is upstairs.

The striped _____ on the walls makes Sandy dizzy.

The band played music as the _____ game began.

You can barely see the _____ insect in the grass.

Mike seems so much _____ that Grandma thinks he must have grown an inch last year.

X it.

The tallest rabbit was stuck in the hallway.	☐	
The rabbit sitting on a small haystack is talking to itself.	☐	
The team was covered with chalk after the game.	☐	
The baseball team used the chalkboard to plan the next game.	☐	
The wallpaper may fall into the bathtub.	☐	
The acrobat walked on top of the wallpaper.	☐	
The pony had a walky-talky inside its stall.	☐	
The stalks beside the window were talking and singing.	☐	
Small bumblebees are flying all over the plate.	☐	
We call to the bumblebees as they buzz near the plane.	☐	
Henry is telling a tall tale while he is walking to the store.	☐	
The tallest teacher gave Henry a talking-to.	☐	
She is calling the smallest robot to come and talk.	☐	
She can recall seeing the smallest robot in an airplane.	☐	

Write it, using a word with *-all* or *-alk*.

	_____
	_____
	_____
	_____
	_____
	_____
	_____

Lesson 4

Words that end in *-old, -olt,* or *-oll* say /ō/ as in *cold*.

Read, write, and ⬭ it.

old			
_____			
told			
_____			
gold			
_____			
bold			
_____			
roll			
_____			
scold			
_____			
colt			
_____			

Words that end in *-old*, *-olt*, or *-oll* say /ō/ as in *cold*.

⬭ the word that matches the picture.

troll   or   told?

hall   or   hold?

belt   or   bold?

foam   or   fold?

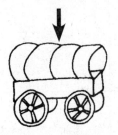 

load   or   old?

stroll   or   salad?

26

	Spell.			Write.
	y h	o a	ld ll	_____
	sc c	a o	le lt	_____
	f t	o a	ll ld	_____
	sm s	o a	ld ll	_____
	n r	e o	ll st	_____
	d c	u o	ld ll	_____
	sh sc	o a	ld lk	_____

27

Yes or no?

	Yes	No
Have you ever molded a sand pile on the beach?	☐	☐
Will a baby colt have a gold saddle?	☐	☐
Would you be scolded if you put a rattlesnake on the stove?	☐	☐
Would you feel cold sitting on top of a snowman?	☐	☐
Can a kitten open a trunk that is bolted shut?	☐	☐
Is it easy to roll up a hill while blowing bubbles?	☐	☐
If you tumble from a bucking colt, will you be jolted?	☐	☐

⬭ the word that matches the picture.

	fold sold cold		troll bald bold
	bolted bowled belted		colder scolding coconut
	bowling basketball wastebasket		rolling molten roping
	older melted molded		potluck potholder ponytail
	goldfish goldfinch goddess		oldest collapse coldest

29

Pick the best word to finish each sentence.

jolted	goldfish	unbolt
oldest	bolder	molded
potholder	folding	retold

Nick is neatly _____ all of the sheets.

You will get bumped and _____ riding on a bucking bronco.

The tall chest will open if we _____ the lock.

When you reach for a hot skillet, you may need to use a _____.

We all loved to hear the fairy tale so Father _____ it.

The human being who has lived the longest is the _____.

After swimming across the pond a second time, I felt stronger and _____.

X it.

Dickey rows the boat under the picnic table.	☐	
Dicky rode the colt to the stable and bolted the gate shut.	☐	
The boldest troll sold the gold earrings to a queen.	☐	
The queen scolded the lad for stealing the gold.	☐	
Betsy retold the tale of the old dragon.	☐	
Betsy sold the old dragon stale cupcakes.	☐	
All the goldfish are swimming to the feast.	☐	
The fish is swinging from the gold seaweed.	☐	
Gretchen was jolted when she fell from the grasshopper.	☐	
Gretchen hopped in the grass and bolted the stall gate shut.	☐	
The monster is walking on a potholder in the sky.	☐	
The flying potholder may give the monster a jolt.	☐	
The team remembers to give Chip all the balls.	☐	
Chip is the tallest member of the basketball team.	☐	

Write it, using a word with *-old*, *-olt*, or *-oll*.

	_____
	_____
	_____
	_____
	_____
	_____
	_____

32

Lesson 5

Words that end in *-ild* or *-ind* may say /ī/ as in *child*.

Read, write, and ⟨⟩ it.

find			
_____			
blindfold			
_____			
wild			
_____			
kind			
_____			
rind			
_____			
mild			
_____			
wind			
_____			

Words that end in *-ild* or *-ind* may say /ī/ as in *ch__ild__*.

⬭ the word that matches the picture.

 fin or find?	 mine or mind?
 hide or hind?	 mild or wild?
 wide or wind?	 blind or blink?
 kind or kite?	chill or child?

	w m	i e	ne nd	_____
	h k	e i	nd ck	_____
	sh ch	i u	t ld	_____
	t f	e i	nd st	_____
	r bl	i e	d nd	_____
	w m	e i	lt ld	_____
	n m	o i	nd ds	_____

Yes or no?

	Yes	No
Will I ever find a needle in a tall haystack?	☐	☐
Does a windup truck need gas from a gas pump?	☐	☐
Is it childish to have a tantrum in the hall?	☐	☐
Can you hide behind a tree?	☐	☐
Would you mind brushing your teeth with cold grated lemon rind?	☐	☐
Can a nasty tiger be wilder than a little puppy?	☐	☐
Can you find an old dragon near your home?	☐	☐

the word that matches the picture.

kingly kindly minding	mindful remind windup
window wilted winding	hiding binding grinding
blondest blindfold blender	swelter minding wildness
leading finding holding	behold behind beheld
childlike chilled hindmost	bottle bolder bolted

Pick the best word to finish each sentence.

finders-keepers	behind	winding
remind	wildly	blinder
childish	kindness	mild

The kittens act like tigers when you play _____.

If you find the kite _____ the trunk, you can play with it.

_____ is a hide-and-seek game.

We call him _____ if he acts like his baby brother.

She is _____ up the robot so it will begin walking.

If you show your dog _____, it will be a faithful pal.

We find it fun to go swimming on a clear and _____ day.

X it.

The wild colt will try to leap over the fence pole.	☐	
If the bolt falls out, the fence will fall.	☐	
The child was walking behind the goldfish.	☐	
The gold ring is talking to the child.	☐	
She finds an old windup train in the hall.	☐	
All kinds of balls are sold by the dog trainer.	☐	
Andy and Steve were blinded by the falling snowballs.	☐	
It was unkind of Steve to call Andy an oddball.	☐	
The child finds a potholder on the sidewalk.	☐	
The pile of lemon rinds is taller than the child.	☐	
Susan talks kindly to her goldfish as she feeds them.	☐	
Susan does not mind feeding all five golden cats.	☐	
The puppet slid the bolt to open the trunk filled with gold.	☐	
The puppy opens the trunk and finds a wild colt.	☐	

Write it, using a word with *-ild,* or *-ind*.

	_____
	_____
	_____
	_____
	_____
	_____
	_____

Lesson 6 • Review Lesson

-all say /all/ as in *ball*.
-alk says /awk/ as in *walk*.
Words that end in *-old, -olt,* or *-oll* say /ō/ as in *cold*.
Words that end in *-ild* or *-ind* say /ī/ as in *child*.

Read, write, and ◯ it.

sidewalk _____			
seat belt _____			
chalkboard _____			
blindfold _____			
roller coaster _____			
smallest _____			
cold cuts _____			

-*all* say /all/ as in *b<u>all</u>*.
-*alk* says /awk/ as in *w<u>alk</u>*.
Words that end in -*old*, -*olt*, or -*oll* say /ō/ as in *c<u>old</u>*.
Words that end in -*ild* or -*ind* say /ī/ as in *ch<u>ild</u>*.

the word that matches the picture.

coldest   or   scolded?

winding   or   wildest?

meatballs   or   baseballs?

overhear   or   overalls?

holding   or   goldfish?

talking   or   tallest?

bold   or   bowl?

postpone   or   potholder?

Spell.   Write.

	ever over	alls ills	_____
	side base	walk wall	_____
	pass base	ball hall	_____
	blank blind	roll fold	_____
	gold sold	fish dish	_____
	beast seat	let belt	_____
	team meat	balls call	_____

Yes or no?

	Yes	No
Will an octopus keep a goldfish in a fishtank?	☐	☐
Can you find cold cuts and cheese in a sandwich?	☐	☐
Are you fearful of a small kitten playing nearby?	☐	☐
Can a pilot wind up and pitch a fastball on the sidewalk?	☐	☐
Is a frisky colt smaller than a little meatball?	☐	☐
Will a wild tiger call your dentist this year?	☐	☐
Would you be scolded for chopping up the peach tree?	☐	☐

⬭ the word that matches the picture.

falling yearlong yearling		retold molded folded	
mindful kindly wildly		overact overalls overthrow	
coldness boldness collect		bolting scolding scroll	
mildness kindness mindless		calling chalked clashing	
raisin brainless rainfall		remind unkind behind	

45

Pick the best word to finish each sentence.

folder	childish	overalls
grindstone	dining hall	winding
blindfold	rollerblades	leap year

Lots of students can eat lunch in a _____.

_____ gives us an extra day in the winter every four years.

It is fun coasting on the sidewalk with _____ on your feet.

When you finish your math papers, put them in your _____.

The children wore _____ to keep clean when they were painting the shed.

To refuse to try things like spinach, peas, or beets is _____.

She is _____ the string into a big ball.

X it.

The meatballs are hidden in a box behind the wall.	☐	
The child spilled meatballs in the hallway.	☐	
The big glass bowl is filled with goldfish.	☐	
The nasty colt is drinking from the goldfish bowl.	☐	
Glen told a tall tale while he ate a meatball sub.	☐	
Glen sold stacks of cold cuts while talking on his phone.	☐	
It is silly to drive unless you use seatbelts.	☐	
The angry driver is yelling at the clanging bell.	☐	
The child did not like the chops at all.	☐	
Tiny mothballs were hung in the closet to protect the clothing.	☐	
Becky was giving her clumsy pet a talking-to.	☐	
The talking pet walks on the sidewalk behind Becky.	☐	
The silly baseball player puts on a blindfold.	☐	
The puppy sits in the bleachers for the baseball game.	☐	

Write it.

	_____
	_____
	_____
	_____
	_____
	_____
	_____

Lesson 7

qu says /kw/ as in _qu_een.

Read, write, and it.

quack			
_____			

quiet			
_____			

quilt			
_____			

gum			
_____			

quick			
_____			

gift			
_____			

quill			
_____			

qu says /kw/ as in <u>queen</u>.

( ) the word that matches the picture.

quack   or   quick?

quiver   or   quarrel?

quail   or   pail?

quite   or   quiet?

quench   or   punch?

quest   or   quart?

quill   or   quilt?

quickly   or   quicksand?

	gu qu	o il	t te	_____
	qu cu	ee e	r n	_____
	k qu	o i	et te	_____
	g qu	e a	rt ck	_____
	qu c	i ai	ck ng	_____
	g qu	u i	ft st	_____
	qu h	i e	ll lp	_____

	Yes	No
Would a real queen quit her job?	☐	☐
When five players make music, is it a quintet?	☐	☐
Can a quail use a quill pen and ink on paper?	☐	☐
Of your teacher gives a quiz, will you get an A+?	☐	☐
Will you quarrel with someone who says that you cheated?	☐	☐
Are you a quitter if you leave the team when it is behind?	☐	☐
Can a duck quack quietly?	☐	☐

the word that matches the picture.

quicksand quickly quicksilver	groaning grown-up quoted
sequel sea gull sea green	quietness quickly quitter
squeak quicken squid	linger liquid licked
acquit acquainted quilt	square squatted squint
$2 + 2 = 4$ equal equip eagle	squeeze squeal square

53

Pick the best word to finish each sentence.

quicksand	squinting	squeezing
liquids	squeaked	quarreled
quietly	quiver	quacking

When Grandpa is sleeping, the children must play
_____.

_____ is soft, wet sand that can swallow up people and animals.

The door _____ as if someone were sneaking inside.

Water and milk are both _____.

Do you hear the _____ of the wild ducks?

Myron is _____ lemons to make lemonade.

The selfish children _____ over the candy.

X it.

The quintet played the music quietly.	☐	
Jack squeezed the box, and squeaky music came out.	☐	
The quail is eating oatmeal on the window sill.	☐	
The man is mixing oatmeal with a quill pen.	☐	
The quick-witted queen saved the child from the wild beast.	☐	
The quick child shows the queen a trick with a cane.	☐	
The shack was standing next to the quicksand.	☐	
You must be quick to catch a quart of rain in your cap.	☐	
The quarreling children squeal and run when Dad drives up.	☐	
The children quarrel over the squealing pig.	☐	
The queen is making a square table with old boxes and boards.	☐	
The queen squeezed the wet quilt and hung it up to dry.	☐	
The winner of the quiz show squealed when she won the prize.	☐	
Isabel quit her job when she had no more equipment.	☐	

Write it, using a word with *qu*.

	_____
	_____
	_____
	_____
	_____
	_____
	_____

Lesson 8

thr says /thr/ as in <u>throne</u>.
shr says /shr/ as in <u>shrink</u>.
scr says /scr/ as in <u>scrub</u>.

Read, write, and ⬭ it.

scrub _____			
screen _____			
throat _____			
scratch _____			
shrub _____			
thrill _____			
scream _____			

thr says /thr/ as in <u>thr</u>one.
shr says /shr/ as in <u>shr</u>ink.
scr says /scr/ as in <u>scr</u>ub.

⬭ the word that matches the picture.

throng   or   throw?

shrubs   or   scrubs?

chug   or   shrug?

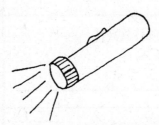

shone   or   thrown?

script   or   shrimp?

scrape   or   shape?

thrill   or   thing?

shrine   or   shrink?

Spell.   Write.

	str thr	o i	ng ne	_____
	scr shr	e ee	n d	_____
	shr spr	i a	mp nk	_____
	thr sh	u i	st ne	_____
	shr thr	oa i	nk t	_____
	scr str	a ea	p m	_____
	shr scr	u a	p b	_____

59

Yes or no?

	Yes	No
Is a three-decker sandwich with potato chips a small snack?	☐	☐
If he screams shrilly all the time, will his throat get sore?	☐	☐
Do you use chalk in class to scribble on the chalkboard?	☐	☐
Could you find a thrift shop that sold wild shrimp?	☐	☐
Should she throw away things all over the shrubs?	☐	☐
Do you mind scrambling up the hill to throw the ball?	☐	☐
If your clothing gets damp and shrinks, does it get smaller?	☐	☐

60

 the word that matches the picture.

 scrap scribble script	 threshold stowaway sore throat
shriveled shrinking shredded wheat	 thinnest thrifty thresh
 scratched scrambled eggs crumbled	 threescore thrilling thriftiest
 threepenny twenty-three twentieth	 screened screeched scratched
 shrillest children chilliness	 throwing thruway thunder

61

Pick the best word to finish each sentence.

screech	three-base hit	shrimp cocktail
thrilling	screens	thrift shop
shrunk	shredded	scribble

Anything that has _____ is much smaller.

If you visit a _____, you will find clothing sold cheaply.

We keep _____ on the windows so insects will not enter.

A little child likes to _____ with chalk on the chalkboard.

If a baseball player gets a _____, the fans may scream.

When a speeding truck stops quickly, its brakes _____.

It is _____ to watch the acrobat on the trapeze.

X it.

The three kids scrambled over the shrubs.	☐	
The three children played a thrilling game with bubbles.	☐	
She scratched her wild rattlesnake on the neck.	☐	
She finds the gold pillow shredded by her pet.	☐	
The three wild ducks did not mind the scratching cats.	☐	
Mitch scrambled up the rocks to find the hot rod.	☐	
The kids were scrubbing the thrift shop.	☐	
The old books in the thrift shop were covered with scribbles.	☐	
A shrinking clown walked behind the throne.	☐	
The throne was shrinking behind the tall shrubs.	☐	
You can hear them thrashing behind the screen.	☐	
It was thrilling to hear the child read the script.	☐	
The shrimp scrambled to make a three-base hit.	☐	
The shrimp is scrubbing itself while sitting on the throne.	☐	

63

Write it, using a word with *thr*, *shr*, or *scr*.

3	_____
(shrimp)	_____
(screen)	_____
(father and son)	_____
(throne)	_____
(boy scrubbing)	_____
(throat)	_____

Lesson 9

str says /str/ as in _strong_.
spr says /spr/ as in _spray_.
spl says /spl/ as in _split_.

Read, write, and ⬭ it.

sprain _____			
split _____			
street _____			
sprint _____			
stripe _____			
splash _____			
strainer _____			

str says /str/ as in *st**r**ong*.
spr says /spr/ as in *sp**r**ay*.
spl says /spl/ as in *sp**l**it*.

⬭ the word that matches the picture.

sprig   or   spring?

scream   or   stream?

splint   or   spit?

splash   or   flush?

strong   or   string?

sprang   or   sprain?

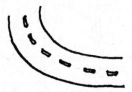

stray   or   street?

spent   or   spleen?

Spell.   Write.

	spl str	a i	t ng	_____
	str spl	a ee	sh t	_____
	st spr	a i	g ng	_____
	sp spl	ea a	k sh	_____
	str tr	i ea	p m	_____
	spr str	a i	y pe	_____
	tr str	ai o	m ng	_____

Yes or no?

	Yes	No
Are you asleep when you spring across the street?	☐	☐
Do you feel cold after splashing in the stream?	☐	☐
Can you play basketball if you sprain your ankle badly?	☐	☐
Would it be splendid to find a tiger in the kitchen?	☐	☐
Should you be strong to dive from a springboard?	☐	☐
In the springtime do sprinkles of rain help string beans to grow?	☐	☐
Will Jacob feel grand if he strikes and misses the ball in the baseball game?	☐	☐

the word that matches the picture.

stronger stroller strainer	sparkle springing sprinkle
spitting spelling splitting	streamer steamer stronger
springtime springboard sputter	spending strengthen splendid
stagger struggle snuggle	splatter platter stutter
sprinting splitting splinter	stretch scratch stitch

Pick the best word to finish each sentence.

strainer	split-level	splatter
springtime	stretcher	strengthen
spraying	stripes	splashing

Do not _____ paint on the windows when you paint the walls.

_____ is the season of the year when leaves begin to grow.

You can _____ your body by sprinting home each day.

Grass will grow tall if you keep _____ it with a hose.

You must walk up steps inside a _____ home.

The happy baby is giggling and _____ in the bathtub.

The American flag has red and white _____.

X it.

Sentences		Picture
The painters were spray-painting the bus.	☐	
The student sprang onto the streamlined bus.	☐	
The string beans are covered with splendid stripes.	☐	
The splendid balls of string are yellow.	☐	
The child struck home plate with the baseball bat.	☐	
The truck splattered mud on the child.	☐	
The puppet's strings are twisted and tangled.	☐	
The big sprinklers spray the puppy.	☐	
The triplets are sprinting beside the cold stream.	☐	
The triplets sprang away from the stroller.	☐	
The logs splash into the nearby stream.	☐	
David is splitting logs on the long dock.	☐	
Chuck splashes into the water from the springboard.	☐	
Dripping wet, Chuck was put on a stretcher.	☐	

Write it, using a word with *str*, *spr*, or *spl*.

	_____
	_____
	_____
	_____
	_____
	_____
	_____

Lesson 10

-*ey* at the end of a word says /ē/ as in *k<u>ey</u>*.

Read, write, and ⬭ it.

honey _____			
chimney _____			
monkey _____			
pulley _____			
valley _____			
donkey _____			
hockey stick _____			

-ey at the end of a word says /ē/ as in *k<u>ey</u>*.

◯ the word that matches the picture.

jelly or jockey?

thrilled or trolley?

lackey or lucky?

valley or varnish?

drummer or donkey?

money or moan?

homer or honey?

chimney or chicken?

	Spell		Write
	stock hock	ing ey	_____
	moan mon	er ey	_____
	dig kid	ger ney	_____
	chim chill	ney y	_____
	ban don	key ner	_____
	hon honk	ing ey	_____
	mon num	key ber	_____

Yes or no?

	Yes No
Does honey fall from the sky when it rains?	☐ ☐
Would a jockey ride a wild colt up the chimney?	☐ ☐
Can a cub scramble up a tree to find a hive full of honey?	☐ ☐
Do monkeys have a grand time throwing peanuts?	☐ ☐
Can a donkey trot across the street to catch a trolley?	☐ ☐
Do you pay money for tickets to see a hockey game?	☐ ☐
Could I tug on a pulley and lift up the sidewalk?	☐ ☐

	hopscotch homemade honeybees		moment money bag Monday
	volunteer volcano volleyball		kindness kidding kidney
	jockey hobby hockey stick		keystone keyhole keynote
	monument monkey moment		trolley tropical stroller
	chimney chimes chimpanzee		seventeen seventy-three several

Pick the best word to finish each sentence.

kidney beans	hockey stick	donkeys
money bags	honeybees	key chain
chimney	volleyball	monkey

Small _____ are buzzing by the beehive.

To make a three-bean salad, you need string beans, yellow beans, and _____.

If you are jumping, swinging, and playing tricks, you may be acting like a _____.

To make a goal, the player strikes the puck with the _____.

Please help me unlock the gate by finding my key on this _____.

Smoke comes out of the _____ when we light the fireplace.

The bank robbers tossed the _____ into the truck and sped away.

X it.

The jockey is holding onto the brass pulley.	☐	
The hockey player is talking with the splendid colt.	☐	
The silly child waves from the trolley window.	☐	
The child uses a key to wind up the hockey game.	☐	
Smokey has a bucket of honey stuck on his nose.	☐	
The strong crocodile eats up the wallet of money.	☐	
A monkey springs from the tallest chimney.	☐	
The monkey stands holding the volleyball.	☐	
Which bottle holds more honey?	☐	
The grown-up on the chimney takes the child's hand.	☐	
A donkey naps near the shredded wheat.	☐	
The honey is spilled all over the kitchen table.	☐	
The hockey stick springs from the player's hand.	☐	
The jockey swings a long key chain in the air.	☐	

Write it, using a word with -ey.

	_____
	_____
	_____
	_____
	_____
	_____
	_____

80

Read, write, and ⬭ it.

sprayed _____			
throwing _____			
rolled _____			
splashed _____			
brushed _____			
quiet _____			
spelled _____			

-ed at the end of a word can say /ĕd/, /d/, or /t/.

◯ the word that matches the picture and ◯ the sound *-ed* makes. The first one is done for you.

walled or (walked)? ed (t) d	twinkled or twisted? ed t d
nailed or mailed? ed t d	vanished or banished? ed t d
blanked or blended? ed t d	called or smelled? ed t d
cramped or stamped? ed t d	brushed or rushed? ed t d

Spell.   Write.

	brain rain	er ed	_____
	cold fold	ed est	_____
	don bang	ed key	_____
	small spell	est ed	_____
	splin splash	ed ter	_____
	win twist	ed tery	_____
	splen stroll	did er	_____

83

Yes or no?

	Yes	No
Does six added to ten equal fifteen?	☐	☐
Would you be pleased if it rained after you had planted seeds?	☐	☐
Will you be angry if you are pinched by your sister?	☐	☐
Would you chase a penny if it rolled on the sidewalk?	☐	☐
Would a panther be thanked if it grabbed all the pancakes?	☐	☐
Would a plate be smashed if it were dropped from a truck?	☐	☐
Would you be thrilled to ride on a roller coaster?	☐	☐

( ) the word that matches the picture.

folders following flowed	escape erased erupted
blindfold blinked blistered	politeness politics polished
subtracted suspected submitted	smelled spelled splashed
transplant travelers propeller	constant constructed continued
whiskers whimpered whispered	valleys vanished famished

85

Pick the best word to finish each sentence.

sprained	connected	polished
brushed	repaired	inspected
belonged	locked	talked

After the silver tray was _____, it was shiny.

He tripped playing baseball and _____ his ankle.

The legs were _____ to the puppet with strings.

Sal called a pal from home, and they _____ a long time.

Fay was trying to find the skates that _____ to her.

When the broken table was fixed, the wobbly chairs were also _____.

They cannot get inside if the gate is _____.

X it.

The teacher asked Josh if he could read the spelling list.	☐	
Josh reached for a napkin after he spilled the lemonade.	☐	
The monkey rushed to the peanuts and opened them.	☐	
The children brushed the donkey's mane and braided its tail.	☐	
The butterfly folded up its wings and napped.	☐	
Sandy folded the blankets on the bed.	☐	
Lee inspected the small buckets of honey.	☐	
Lee collected a small bundle of money.	☐	
Patsy splashed pink punch all over her clean dress.	☐	
Patsy punched her pillow and tossed it at her sister.	☐	
The rabbits hopped away to find sweet clover.	☐	
The rabbit was scolded for stealing the money.	☐	
The talented class presented a play.	☐	
The class displayed all the paintings.	☐	

Write it.

	_____
	_____
	_____
	_____
	_____
	_____
	_____

(Teacher dictated. See Key for Books 1 to 5.)

⬭ the word you hear.

1.	childless chilliness childlike childish chicken	2.	sideline sideways sidewalk sideswipe sidetrack
3.	connector contented conquered connived connected	4.	streaky streamlined steeliness streamlet steamer
5.	billing billion billow blinked billboard	6.	shuffleboard shrugging shrinkable shudder shrunken
7.	halfway halted hallway shallow hallow	8.	contacted combat concluded conducted conducting
9.	behave behind behold blinded beheld	10.	insider instant insulted inspected inspired

Book 5 — Posttest

(Teacher dictated. See Key for Books 1 to 5.)

1. _____

   _____

2. _____

   _____

3. _____

   _____

4. _____

   _____

5. _____

   _____

6. _____

   _____

Read, and then write the word.

1. In winter I use mittens so my hands will not be

   c_____.

2. The members of the team play a game with a

   bat and a b_____.

3. When I throw crackers in the pond, I can hear

   the ducks q_____.

4. In a fairy tale, the queen sits on a golden

   t_____.

5. To open the brass lock I will use a k_____.

6. It is fun to jump in the water and make a big

   s_____.

Use the words to complete the sentences.

gold	mailed	key	quack
behind	springs	bolt	child

1. On a rainy day the _____ sneaks up to the attic. He spots a dusty trunk hidden _____ the chimney. He slides the _____ to try to open the trunk, but he needs a _____ as well. He finds it and quickly unlocks the trunk. The top of the trunk _____ open. Is it filled with gold?

cold cuts	stall	money	splendid
kindly	hold	screamed	roller coaster

2. It was a _____ day at the fair. All the children got tickets to ride on the _____. They had to _____ on so they would not fall. They yelled and _____ as the ride dipped and twisted. Later they had a grand lunch of chips and sandwiches made with _____ and cheese. Needless to say, by the end of the day they had spent all their _____.

honey	clapped	crashed	tallest
thrilled	struck	chalkboard	sold

3. As the hockey team entered the rink, the fans cheered and _____. Then the game began. The players on both teams _____ boldly at the puck with the sticks. All of the players were skating rapidly when suddenly three of them _____ into the side of the rink. The _____ player tripped and fell into the goal. It was a wild game, but the fans were _____ to see the underdog team win!